PRACTICE
ANTHONY BRESCIA

THE WESTERN HERITAGE
VOLUME II -- SINCE 1648

EIGHTH EDITION

Donald Kagan
Frank M. Turner
Steven Ozment

Upper Saddle River, New Jersey 07458

© 2004 by PEARSON EDUCATION, INC.
Upper Saddle River, New Jersey 07458

All rights reserved

10 9 8 7 6 5 4 3 2 1

ISBN 0-13-182862-2

Printed in the United States of America

CONTENTS

13	Paths To Constitutionalism And Absolutism: England And France In The Seventeenth Century	1
14	New Directions in Thought and Culture in the Sixteenth and Seventeenth Centuries	5
15	Successful and Unsuccessful Paths to Power (1686–1740)	9
16	Society and Economy Under the Old Regime in the Eighteenth Century	13
17	The Transatlantic Economy, Trade Wars, and Colonial Rebellion	17
18	The Age of Enlightenment: Eighteenth-Century Thought	21
19	The French Revolution	25
20	The Age of Napoleon and the Triumph of Romanticism	29
21	The Conservative Order and the Challenges of Reform (1815-1832)	33
22	Economic Advance and Social Unrest (1830-1850)	37
23	The Age of Nation-States	41
24	The Building of European Supremacy: Society and Politics to World War I	45
25	The Birth of Modern European Thought	49
26	Imperialism, Alliances, and War	54
27	Political Experiments of the 1920s	58

28	Europe and the Great Depression of the 1930s	62
29	World War II	66
30	The Cold War and the Emergence of the New Europe	70
31	The West at the Dawn of the Twenty-First Century	74

| Lecture Companion | 78 |
| Answer Key | 98 |

Chapter 13
PATHS TO CONSTITUTIONALISM AND ABSOLUTISM: ENGLAND AND FRANCE IN THE SEVENTEENTH CENTURY

Multiple-Choice

1. The book, A Trew Law of Free Monarchies was written by
    (a) James VI of Scotland.
    (b) John Locke.
    (c) Charles I.
    (d) Oliver Cromwell.

2. The 1604 conference at Hampton Court established the basis of the
    (a) Plymouth colony.
    (b) Millenary Petition
    (c) Scottish presbytery
    (d) none of the above

3. Whom of the following was least supportive of English monarchial government in the period 1620 through the 1640s?
    (a) the duke of Buckingham
    (b) John Hampden
    (c) Thomas Wentworth
    (d) William Laud

4. The so-called Test Act was largely aimed at discrediting
    (a) Titus Oates.
    (b) James, duke of York.
    (c) Charles II.
    (d) Earl of Shaftsbury.

5. The reason for the continuing opposition to the reign of James 11 was his
    (a) imprisonment of Anglican bishops.
    (b) appointments of known Catholics to high offices.
    (c) insistence upon the repeal of the Test Act.
    (d) all of the above

6. _____ was least directly responsible for the establishment of absolutism in France during, the seventeenth century.
    (a) Louis XIII
    (b) Sully
    (c) Richelieu
    (d) Mazarin

7. Jansenists believed that
    (a) original sin had been redeemed through Christ's death.
    (b) Cornelis Jansen should be canonized.
    (c) original sin could not be redeemed without special grace from God.
    (d) St. Augustine had incorrectly interpreted the concept of original sin.

8. The marquis of Louvois is noted for
    (a) establishing a professional French army.
    (b) his superior military tactics
    (c) introducing a merit-based system of promotion within the French army.
    (d) all of the above

9. Louis XIV considered the revocation of the Edict of Nantes
    (a) unimportant.
    (b) militarily significant.
    (c) his most pious act.
    (d) good for business.

10. The correct chronological order of these important treaties negotiated during the wars of Louis XIV would be
    (a) Utrecht-Rastadt, Ryswick, Nijmwegen.
    (b) Nijmwegen, Ryswick, Utrecht-Rastadt.
    (c) Ryswick, Nijmwegen, Aix-la-Chapelle.
    (d) Nijmwegen, Utrecht-Rastadt, Ryswick.

True-False

_____1. John Pym was among the important leaders of Parliament who opposed the policies of Charles I.

_____2. The alliance with Scottish Presbyterians and the reorganization of the army under Parliament assured the Puritan victory over Charles I.

_____3. Charles II of England died a Roman Catholic.

_____4. The English Toleration Act of 1689 granted religious freedom to all but the most radical religious groups.

_____5. Despite his persecution of the Huguenots at home, Cardinal Richelieu allied France with Swedish Protestants during the Thirty Years' War.

_____6. Throughout the seventeenth century, the Catholic Jansenists allied with the Jesuits against French Huguenots.

_____7. Jean-Baptiste Colbert's economic policies had the effect of diminishing France's industrial and commercial potential.

_____ 8. In reality, the revocation of the Edict of Nantes came as a complete surprise.

_____ 9. Philip of Anjou was the grandson of Louis XIV.

_____ 10. From a military perspective, regarding each of the wars fought in the reign of Louis XIV, France was best prepared for the War of Spanish Succession.

Completion

1. James VI of Scotland, who became James I of England, was the son of _____.

2. The religious minister under Charles I was _____ and, in the 1630s, he provoked a war with Scotland.

3. The fate of Charles I appears to have been sealed when Cromwell's New Model Army defeated him at _____ in June 1645.

4. The largest military engagement of the English Civil War was the 1644 battle at _____.

5. _____ was the official title used by Oliver Cromwell after taking power in 1653.

6. The so-called "Glorious Revolution" in England was justified in the work titled Second Treatise on Government written by _____.

7. An involuntary national labor force was created in France in the seventeenth century by the introduction of the royal _____.

8. One of the most important factors in establishing absolutism in France was the systematic reduction of the influence of the _____.

9. The most famous of the defenders of the Jansenist movement was _____.

10. _____ is the name used to describe the financial policies of the French minister Colbert.

Short Answer

1. English politics during the seventeenth century was a blend of religious concerns and monarchial decline. How does the reign of Elizabeth I in the previous century set the stage for the struggle between king and Parliament in this era?

2. What factors do you consider important in assessing the success of the Puritans during Cromwell's era?

3. Assess the roles of Cardinals Richelieu and Mazarin in the establishment of absolutism in France.

4. Examine the reign of Louis XIV. What were his successes and what were his failures?

5. Compare and contrast the development of the governments of England and France during the seventeenth century. Answer with specific references to persons, statutes, and events as needed.

Chapter 14
NEW DIRECTIONS IN THOUGHT AND CULTURE IN THE SIXTEENTH AND SEVENTEENTH CENTURIES

Multiple-Choice
1. Which of the following expressions best characterizes the nature of the Scientific Revolution?
    (a) It occurred several places in Europe at the same time.
    (b) It was not revolutionary in the normal sense of the word.
    (c) It was a complex movement involving many persons.
    (d) all of the above

2. Whom of the following actually opposed Copernicus's views?
    (a) Tycho Brahe
    (b) Johannes Kepler
    (c) Galileo Galilei
    (d) Francis Bacon.

3. The harmony between faith and science in this period is found in which of these views?
    (a) Since nature is reasonable, God must be reasonable.
    (b) To study the laws of nature in reality is to study God.
    (c) Faith and science are mutually supporting.
    (d) all of the above

4. Whom of the following popularized the Copernican system and articulated the concept of a universe subject to mathematical laws?
    (a) Galileo
    (b) Bacon
    (c) Locke
    (d) Kepler

5. The belief that human knowledge should produce useful results was held by
    (a) Francis Bacon.
    (b) Johannes Kepler.
    (c) Descartes.
    (d) none of the above

6. Analytic geometry was first developed by
    (a) Galileo.
    (b) Brahe.
    (c) Descartes.
    (d) none of the above

7. Pascal believed that
    (a) there was danger in following traditional religious ways.
    (b) misery loves company.
    (c) God's mercy was for everyone.
    (d) it is better to believe in God than not to.

8. The religious thought associated with deducing of religious conclusions from nature became known as
    (a) econo-theology.
    (b) naturo-theology.
    (c) physico-theology.
    (d) none of the above

9. In Thomas Hobbes's view, man was
    (a) a person neither good nor evil.
    (b) a self-centered beast.
    (c) essentially God-fearing.
    (d) none of the above

10. Which of the following works was written first?
    (a) On the Revolutions of Heavenly Spheres
    (b) The New Astronomy
    (c) Leviathan
    (d) Ethics

True-False

_____1. Nicolaus Copernicus found the Ptolemaic system of the universe to be mathematically clumsy and inconsistent.

_____2. Middle-aged and older women were particularly vulnerable during this era of witch hunts.

_____3. Tycho Brahe advocated an earth-centered system to astronomy.

_____4. Galileo popularized the Copernican system and articulated the concept of a universe subject to mathematical laws.

_____5. The proponents of the new science sought to explain the world in terms of mechanical metaphors, or the language of machinery.

_____6. The Englishman Francis Bacon is considered to be the founder of empiricism and experimentation in science.

_____7. In 1632, René Descartes wrote Dialogues on the Two Chief Systems of the World.

____8. The Jansenists believed in the total sinfulness of humans, their eternal predestination, and their dependence on grace for salvation.

____9. In the seventeenth century, no one really believed in the power of demons.

____10. Thomas Hobbes supported the idea of a strong and efficient ruler because he believed such a ruler would alleviate the dangers for humans existing in the state of nature.

Completion
1. The Ptolemaic view of the universe is found in a work written in the second century and titled the _____ .

2. The work of _____ expanded on the previous efforts of Nicolaus Copernicus and Tycho Brahe.

3. For Galileo, the rationality for the entire universe was based on _____ .

4. The work of _____ focused on the issue of planetary motion and established a basis for physics.

5. _____ invented analytic geometry.

6. In the Leviathan, _____ portrayed human beings and society in a thoroughly materialistic and mechanical way.

7. As an intellectual, _____ compared himself to Christopher Columbus.

8. The political philosopher Thomas Hobbes believed that the dangers of _____ were greater than the dangers of tyranny.

9. _____ was the author of Grounds of Natural Philosophy.

10. _____ believed that human beings were capable of goodwill and rational behavior.

Short Answer
1. Describe the roles of Nicolaus Copernicus and Francis Bacon in influencing what is now referred to as the Scientific Revolution.

2. What was the new worldview worked out during this era? How did it differ from the medieval view? What effects did the new concept of the universe have on all of the sciences?

3. Discuss the central characteristics of the thought of Thomas Hobbes. Are there parts of his work that are reflected in modern times?

4. Contrast Hobbes's view of authority with that of John Locke. Why is Locke considered so influential even in modern times?

Chapter 15
SUCCESSFUL AND UNSUCCESSFUL PATHS TO POWER (1686–1740)

Multiple-Choice

1. According to the text, which of the following countries was not moving forward in this period?
    - (a) Great Britain
    - (b) Russia
    - (c) Spain
    - (d) Prussia

2. Which of the following contributed least to the decline of the Netherlands in the eighteenth century?
    - (a) the fishing industry
    - (b) shipbuilding
    - (c) the financial community
    - (d) various domestic industries

3. The Mississippi Company
    - (a) after earlier troubles operated profitably.
    - (b) was responsible for the management of the French national debt.
    - (c) ended the financial career of John Law.
    - (d) all of the above

4. During the eighteenth century, the English Parliament was dominated by
    - (a) the old aristocracy.
    - (b) the rising middle class.
    - (c) owners of property.
    - (d) representatives of the people.

5. As one moved farther eastward in Europe in the eighteenth century, there was increasing likelihood of finding
    - (a) rotten boroughs.
    - (b) serfdom.
    - (c) prominent intellectuals.
    - (d) larger navies.

6. During this period of time, Sweden's weakness was in her
    - (a) economy
    - (b) army
    - (c) location on the Baltic Sea
    - (d) none of the above

7. In the early eighteenth century a major defeat of Sweden occurred in the battle of
    (a) Poltava.
    (b) Regensburg.
    (c) Narva.
    (d) none of the above

8. Beginning in this era, a major factor in European international relations was the decline of
    (a) the Ottoman Empire.
    (b) Poland.
    (c) Russia.
    (d) Austria.

9. The General-Ober-Finanz-Kriegs-und-Domänen-Direktorium is normally associated with the state of
    (a) Russia.
    (b) Poland.
    (c) Prussia.
    (d) the Holy Roman Empire.

10. Which of the following occurred first?
    (a) Russia defeated in the battle at Narva
    (b) European tour of Peter the Great
    (c) Saint Petersburg founded
    (d) end of the Great Northern War

True-False

_____1. The Netherlands won its independence from Spain in the Treaty of Westphalia.

_____2. The chief feature of French political life in the eighteenth century until the French Revolution (1789) was the attempt of the nobility to limit monarchial power.

_____3. Louis XV of France is considered a failure not only because of his mediocrity, but because he was never properly trained as a ruler, was lazy, and given to vice.

_____4. Both Whigs and Tories were proponents of the status quo in England, yet the Tories supported urban commercial interests and were in favor of religious toleration in general.

_____5. Control of the House of Commons could be achieved by the careful use of patronage and electoral management of the boroughs in England.

_____6. By the end of the seventeenth century, warfare and the resultant shifting political alliances had become basic ingredients of life in central Europe.

_____ 7. The Pragmatic Sanction was designed to ensure the succession to the Austrian throne of Maria Theresa.

_____ 8. The Hohenzollern rulers of Prussia received the title of King, in recognition of the marriage of Frederick William I to Maria Theresa.

_____ 9. As a result of frequent revolutions, military conspiracies, and assassinations the Romanovs ruled Russia for only 100 years.

_____ 10. By the middle of the eighteenth century, Russia was Europe's largest producer of iron.

Completion

1. The Netherlands emerged as a nation after revolting against _____ in 1572.

2. Though not having the power to legislate, the _____ of France became effective centers of resistance to royal authority.

3. The most influential minister in the reign of France's Louis XV was the aged _____.

4. In reality _____ could be considered the first Prime Minister of Great Britain.

5. By laying siege to the city of _____ in 1683, the Turks were able to demonstrate the power of the Ottoman Empire.

6. The liberiim veto was a practice exercised in the central legislative assembly of _____.

7. The rise of the Hohenzollern family to control of Prussia began with their rule of the German territory of _____.

8. _____ were the important class of German nobility influential throughout Prussian history.

9. In 1722, Peter the Great attempted to rearrange the Russian nobility through the _____.

10. An early attempt at religious reform in Russia was led by the Patriarch _____.

Short Answers

1. Describe the development of parliamentary government in England in the first half of the eighteenth century. What kind of compromises made this unique system work?

2. How does the development of central authority in Prussia differ from that in other European states during this period? How was it similar?

3. Why were the so-called "reform" efforts of Russia's Peter the Great successful only in part?

4. Generally characterize the differences between the Eastern European states [Sweden, Poland, Austria, Prussia, and Russia] and the Western states [France and England].

5. In a review of the states of eighteenth-century Europe, which one(s) would you consider as showing the most promise for the future, and why?

Chapter 16
SOCIETY AND ECONOMY UNDER THE OLD REGIME IN THE EIGHTEENTH CENTURY

Multiple-Choice

1. According to the textbook, the old regime was characterized by all of the following except
    (a) absolute monarchy.
    (b) the scarcity of food.
    (c) aristocratic elites.
    (d) Protestant domination.

2. The leadership within the British aristocracy was composed of approximately _____ families.
    (a) 200
    (b) 400
    (c) 600
    (d) 800

3. _____ instituted the idea of crop rotation.
    (a) Arthur Young
    (b) Charles Townsend
    (c) Jethro Tull
    (d) Robert Bakewell

4. _____ developed new techniques in animal breeding.
    (a) Robert Bakewell
    (b) Henry Cort
    (c) Arthur Young
    (d) Jethro Tull.

5. Population growth during the eighteenth century appears to be caused mainly by all of the following except
    (a) fewer wars and epidemics.
    (b) better medical knowledge and techniques.
    (c) a decline in the death rate.
    (d) changes in the supply and quality of food.

6. During this century, which of the following was not a contributing factor to Britain's industrial development?
    (a) generally low taxes
    (b) highly stratified class structure
    (c) rich deposits of coal and iron
    (d) few internal trade barriers

7. The machine most responsible for bringing about the combination of industrialization with urbanization was the
    - (a) power loom.
    - (b) flying shuttle.
    - (c) steam engine.
    - (d) spinning jenny.

8. In this era, poverty was
    - (a) worse in the cities.
    - (b) considered a crime.
    - (c) almost nonexistent.
    - (d) worse in the countryside.

9. Which of the following statements is most correct about the emerging middle class in Europe?
    - (a) The land was not a primary source of middle class income.
    - (b) They wanted more regulation of trade and commerce
    - (c) They lived chiefly in the towns and cities.
    - (d) All of these are correct statements about the middle class of this era.

10. Which of the following is least correct about eighteenth-century society?
    - (a) It was on the brink of considerable economic, social, and political change
    - (b) Scarcity remained a major problem throughout western Europe
    - (c) The growth of population was affecting most areas of European life
    - (d) There was a growing willingness among all the classes to seek innovative solutions to all the problems confronted.

True-False

_____1. Oddly, in their desire to protect the status quo, eighteenth-century peasants and aristocracy protected existing privileges.

_____2. Although an important example of what might be called "class legislation," European game laws actually benefited the lower classes.

_____3. The practice of young men and women moving away from home was known as neocolonialism.

_____4. In nonaristocratic households, the males were expected to do virtually all the work of the family unit.

_____5. The eighteenth century saw a stabilization of the numbers of children admitted to foundling homes.

_____6. Though upsetting the political structure, industrialization permitted greater control over the forces of nature than had ever been possible before.

_____ 7. Edmund Cartwright developed the power loom in the 1780s.

_____ 8. Generally, the emerging middle class feared those below them and resented those above them in society.

_____ 9. The Gordon Riots in England were primarily aimed at weakening the Protestant influence in London commerce.

_____ 10. As we know it today, the desire to make money and accumulate profits really began in the eighteenth century.

Completion

1. Eighteenth-century French aristocracy was basically divided into the nobility of the _____ and the nobility of the _____ .

2. Catherine the Great's issuance of the rights and privileges of the Russian nobility gave legal definition to the _____ .

3. _____ constituted the economic basis of eighteenth-century life.

4. The great peasant uprising in Russia during the reign of Catherine the Great was led by _____ .

5. The first practical steam engine was invented by _____ .

6. The new puddling process, which vastly improved the qualities of the iron produced, was developed by _____ .

7. During the eighteenth century, Europe's most populous city was _____ .

8. The engravings of _____ portray the problems caused by alcohol abuse in London during the mid-eighteenth century.

9. Urban _____ during this era were generally well-organized actions against price increases.

10. Throughout the era of the old regime, European _____ were considered socially and religiously inferior.

Short Answer

1. Generally describe the operation of the eighteenth-century nonaristocratic family. How did servants fit into this pattern? Fully describe the role of women in, and without, a family. How did preteen children fit into the world you have described?

2. Discuss the impact of the agricultural and industrial revolutions on working women. Did these revolutions strengthen the role of women in the workforce? Why or why not?

3. A number of newly invented machines were fundamental to the early stages of industrialization. What were these machines, and in what way(s) were they improvements over the previous method of production? How did these machines actually work, and what specific effect did each have on a given process?

4. Why was the comparatively small middle class considered the most dynamic of the eighteenth-century urban classes?

5. To what would you attribute the striking contrast between urban rich and the urban poor in the eighteenth century? How do the distinctions between them reflect the overall problem of urban life then and now?

Chapter 17
THE TRANSATLANTIC ECONOMY, TRADE WARS, AND COLONIAL REBELLION

Multiple-Choice

1. European contacts with the rest of the world have passed through how many distinct stages?
    - (a) 3
    - (b) 4
    - (c) 5
    - (d) 6

2. Which of the following would not be considered a foundation of pre-twentieth century colonial development?
    - (a) national prestige
    - (b) new mineral resources
    - (c) trade
    - (d) military strategy

3. The most influential part of Spain's efforts to control trade with her possessions in the New World was the
    - (a) viceroys.
    - (b) flota system.
    - (c) Casa de Contratación.
    - (d) Peninsulares.

4. Which of the following cities was not a center of the Atlantic slave trade?
    - (a) Amsterdam, Netherlands
    - (b) Liverpool, England
    - (c) Newport, Rhode Island
    - (d) Nantes, France

5. Empress Maria Theresa's arrangement with the _____ preserved the state in the eighteenth century but actually hampered later development.
    - (a) Prussians
    - (b) Turks
    - (c) Poles
    - (d) Magyars

6. Which of the following treaties was negotiated first?
    - (a) Treaty of Paris
    - (b) Treaty of Aix-la-Chapelle
    - (c) Treaty of Westphalia
    - (d) Treaty of Utrecht

7. The root causes of the American colonial revolt against Great Britain was
    (a) concern with imperial taxation.
    (b) concern over imperial policy toward western lands.
    (c) the growth of the colonial economy.
    (d) all of the above

8. Initially, the Second Continental Congress was
    (a) belligerent.
    (b) Promonarchy.
    (c) conciliatory.
    (d) none of the above

9. Which of the following documents had the most effect on the American struggle for independence?
    (a) The Treaty of Paris
    (b) Convention of Westminster
    (c) Common Sense
    (d) The North Briton

10. After the American Revolution, British trade with her former colonies
    (a) stopped altogether.
    (b) increased.
    (c) decreased.
    (d) remained the same.

True-False

_____1. Armies were the most important feature of eighteenth-century mercantile empires.

_____2. Joseph Dupleix and Robert Clive are both important names associated with the European colonization efforts in India.

_____3. For Spain, the governmental structure in the colonies was designed to augment commercial goals.

_____4. Generally speaking, most slave codes were designed to protect those held in bondage from the excessive cruelties of their masters.

_____5. In reality, the British right secured in the Treaty of Utrecht to send one ship per year to the great trading fair at Portobello, Panama opened the door to vast smuggling opportunities.

_____6. The real surprise in the so-called "diplomatic revolution" was the British-French settlement of outstanding colonial differences.

_____7. Throughout his career, Count Anton Kaunitz, the Austrian foreign minister, was determined to maintain a German-based alliance with Prussia.

_____8. The 1773 Tea Act that triggered the Boston Tea Party actually had lowered the price of tea for the colonies.

_____9. The right of taxation, the arbitrary power of the monarchy, and the perceived corruption of the House of Commons were all factors influencing American opinion on the eve of the War of Independence.

_____10. More than ever, the American revolution should be viewed not only as a movement for colonial independence, but one destined to eventually shape the world that followed.

Completion

1. In this period the most valuable of the Dutch colonial possessions was _____.

2. The governing principle behind all colonization was the theory of _____.

3. The area considered to be the most valuable in the eyes of all the European states was the _____.

4. One of the more unusual aspects of Great Britain's rivalry with Spain during this period was a 1739 conflict known as the War of _____.

5. In American colonial history, the Seven Years' War is known as the _____.

6. The British ministry under George Grenville passed the _____ Act which was symbolic of Britain's need for additional revenue.

7. The _____ crisis set the stage for years of struggle between Britain and her American colonies, finally leading to the latter's independence.

8. Political theory that inspired the successful American drive for independence can be found in the writings of _____.

9. _____ was the English monarch throughout the period of the American Revolution.

10. Internal opposition to the king of Great Britain can be associated with the group known as the _____.

Short Answer

1. Describe the mercantile empires of the major European states. What was the particular colonial or economic value of each area?

2. Define mercantilism and give several eighteenth-century examples of the practice.

3. Describe the development of slavery in the New World during this era. Can you distinguish between Spanish and English usage of Africans in their respective colonial empires? Why was France less involved in the slave trade than the other major competitors for the Empire in the New World?

4. Discuss several factors of British life in the 1750s and 1760s which, in your opinion, were stimulants to the rebellion in North America.

5. Discuss the impact of Thomas Paine's *Common Sense* on the American Revolution.

Chapter 18
THE AGE OF ENLIGHTENMENT: EIGHTEENTH-CENTURY THOUGHT

Multiple-Choice

1. Which of the following is the least accurate statement about the philosophes?
    - (a) They were most often men from the upper classes of society.
    - (b) They held a common desire for reform of society, government, and thought
    - (c) They used the printed word as their major weapon.
    - (d) They were not well-organized and disagreed on many points.

2. Which of the following works was not written by Voltaire?
    - (a) Letters on the English
    - (b) The Persian Letters
    - (c) Elements of the Philosophy of Newton
    - (d) Candide

3. The statement, "Crush the Infamous Thing," applies to
    - (a) monarchy.
    - (b) aristocracy.
    - (c) Christianity.
    - (d) all of the above

4. During this period it was argued that the purpose of laws was to achieve
    - (a) justice for all classes.
    - (b) the greatest good for the greatest number.
    - (c) religious toleration for all peoples.
    - (d) none of the above

5. Adam Smith's philosophy of economics basically advocated all but
    - (a) increased tariff regulation.
    - (b) free pursuit of economic self-interest.
    - (c) exploitation of the earth's physical resources.
    - (d) free trade.

6. The foundation of Montesquieu's ideas for reform stem from
    - (a) his study of sociology.
    - (b) his effort to support aristocratic institutions.
    - (c) the inefficient absolutism of monarchy in France.
    - (d) his knowledge of the development of the English cabinet system.

7. Which of the following was not written by Rousseau?
    (a) Nathan the Wise
    (b) (b) The Social Contract
    (c) Discourse on the Moral Effects of the Arts and Sciences
    (d) Discourse on the Origin of Inequality

8. The concept that under certain circumstances some people must be forced to be free is associated with the thinking of
    (a) Rousseau.
    (b) Montesquieu.
    (c) Bentham.
    (d) Locke.

9. Which of the following rulers is not normally associated with the ideas of Enlightened Absolutism?
    (a) Joseph II of Austria
    (b) Catherine the Great of Russia
    (c) George III of England
    (d) Frederick III of Prussia

10. In the last analysis, the Enlightened Monarchs of the eighteenth century supported change and innovation because of their
    (a) need for international prestige.
    (b) desire for increased revenue.
    (c) desire to impress their respective aristocracies.
    (d) none of the above

True-False

_____ 1. A long-term effect of the Enlightenment has been the spirit of innovation and improvement that first took root within Western societies.

_____ 2. John Locke fully accepted the Christian view of humankind flawed by sin.

_____ 3. John Toland's 1696 publication Christianity Not Mysterious became an important defense of medieval Christianity during the Enlightenment.

_____ 4. For the Scottish philosophe David Hume, the greatest miracle of all was the belief in miracles.

_____ 5. Gotthold Lessing's Nathan the Wise actually called for the religious toleration of non-Christians.

_____ 6. François Quesnay headed a French mercantile association opposed to physiocratic thought.

_____ 7. Montesquieu's analysis of the separation of powers within the British constitutional system called attention to the role of patronage and corruption.

_____ 8. Adam Smith wrote that, "All men are born free, but everywhere they are in chains," to call attention to the need for laissez-faire economics.

_____ 9. Mary Wollstonecraft argued that it was in a woman's best interest to be the sensual slave of man.

_____ 10. Leopold II, upon succession to the Austrian throne, made a concerted effort to repudiate some, but not all of the reforms of his brother Joseph II.

Completion

1. In comparison to all others, _____ was the freest country of the eighteenth century.

2. _____ was the journal which encouraged conversation of diverse topics and the reading of books.

3. The publication of the _____ can be considered the greatest literary monument of the Enlightenment era.

4. The idea that was advanced in an attempt to establish a natural and rational base to religion was known as _____ .

5. The Decline and Fall of the Roman Empire was written by _____ .

6. The comment, "first servant of the State," is associated with _____ .

7. The most coldly rational of the so-called Enlightened Absolutists was _____

8. Catherine the Great was of _____ descent.

9. _____ was the title of a set of guidelines issued by Catherine the Great that reflected some of the political ideas of the Enlightenment.

10. During the second half of the eighteenth century, the formal boundaries of _____ were removed from the map of Europe.

Short Answer
1. Explain the concept of deism. How is deism a reflection of Enlightenment thought?

2. Discuss the thinking and work of Baron Montesquieu. In your opinion, what has been the long-term impact of his work?

3. Discuss the thinking and works of Jean Jacques Rousseau. In your opinion, what has been the long-term impact of his work?

4. What is meant by the term Enlightened Absolutism? How is it a reflection of eighteenth-century thought?

5. Generally, how would you describe the overall impact of Enlightenment ideas on Europe? Consider these ideas as reflected in our own society today.

Chapter 19
THE FRENCH REVOLUTION

Multiple-Choice

1. The text notes that the French Revolution had each of the following effects except
    (a) Catholicism in France was seriously challenged.
    (b) the disruption of the Revolution was contained in France
    (c) people of lower birth held wide influence in political and military affairs.
    (d) conscripted armies defeated professionally trained armies.

2. The most able minister to serve Louis XVI was
    (a) Étienne Charles Lomenie de Brienne.
    (b) René Maupeou.
    (c) Jacques Necker.
    (d) Charles Alexandre de Calonne.

3. Which of the following is often considered the document that put an end to the old regime in France?
    (a) The Cahiers
    (b) The Civil Constitution of the Clergy
    (c) The Declaration of the Rights of Man and Citizen
    (d) The Tennis Court Oath

4. After the passage of the Civil Constitution of the Clergy, the Catholic Church in France was _____ to the French Revolution.
    (a) increasingly supportive
    (b) decreasingly supportive
    (c) openly opposed
    (d) none of the above

5. The 1793 revolt in the Vendée was in support of
    (a) the Jacobins.
    (b) the Prussians.
    (c) the monarchy.
    (d) the Girondists.

6. In 1793 the Cathedral of Notre Dame became the
    (a) headquarters of the Jacobin party.
    (b) Temple of Virtue.
    (c) prison of Marie Antoinette.
    (d) Temple of Reason.

7. The approximately 25,000 victims of the Reign of Terror were largely
    (a) lower class.
    (b) clergy.
    (c) aristocracy.
    (d) none of the above

8. By the end of 1795, legislation in France regarding the status of women
    (a) liberalized divorce procedures for them.
    (b) supported their involvement in the political process.
    (c) upgraded their status in the eyes of the Church.
    (d) left them with somewhat less freedom than enjoyed before 1789.

9. The Thermidorean Constitution of the Year III (1795), required that members of the legislature be
    (a) married.
    (b) widowed.
    (c) female.
    (d) none of the above

10. In the latter half of the 1790s, the government of the Directory was primarily supported by
    (a) sans-culottes groups.
    (b) the army.
    (c) the Catholic Church.
    (d) Napoleon Bonaparte.

True-False

_____1. The statement, "What is the Third Estate? Everything," was made by Louis XVI on the eve of convening the French Estates General.

_____2. The "Great Fear" occurred in the summer of 1789 as a result of rumors of coming food shortages.

_____3. One of the major reasons for not immediately repudiating the French national debt was that much of it was owed to the very people represented by the Third Estate.

_____4. The new currency issued by the National Assembly near the end of 1790 was backed by lands confiscated from the aristocracy of France.

_____5. The 1792 massacre of persons in Paris jails came to be known as the "October Days."

_____6. An example of the effect the French Revolution was having on other European states was the burning of Alexander Radishchev's book *Journey from Saint Petersburg to Moscow*.

_____ 7. Lazare Carnot, a prominent Jacobin, was responsible for the organization of republican military armies.

_____ 8. The so-called enrages were a radical group of sans-culottes that urged greater price regulations and a more extreme policy of dechristianization.

_____ 9. The Thermidorean Reaction was chiefly supported by the aristocracy in combination with the sans-culottes.

_____ 10. One of the unanticipated results of the Thermidorean Reaction was a notable revival of Catholicism.

Completion

1. In 1774 _____ became the king of France.

2. The question of _____ procedures remained an unresolved problem in 1788 and during the earliest meetings of the Estates General.

3. The taking of the Bastille resulted in the release of _____ prisoners.

4. The 1791 Declaration of _____ was an effort by the kings of Austria and Prussia to protect the French royal family.

5. The most advanced and best organized political group of the National Constituent Assembly was the _____ .

6. A 1792 Manifesto issued by the _____ had the effect of strengthening French resistance to foreign invasion.

7. The battle of _____ in 1792 is often considered as the victory of democracy over aristocracy.

8. _____ took a position against the French Revolution in his work titled Reflections on the Revolution in France.

9. In some French cities, Jacobins were murdered in the streets during the Thermidorean Reaction by gangs of youths known as the _____ .

10. The term a "whiff of grapeshot" is associated with _____ .

Short Answer

1. Discuss the financial crisis in France on the eve of the French Revolution. Why was the problem so grave in a country that had considerable wealth? Distinguish between the rural and urban aspects of the problem.

2. What were the policies of the National Constituent Assembly toward the Catholic Church? How would these policies "revolutionize" church-state relations throughout Europe?

3. What caused the Reign of Terror in France? Are events such as this normal in revolutionary movements? Was there a similar or comparable situation in the American Revolution?

4. Describe the Thermidorean Reaction. Why should these events be considered as important parts of the era of the French Revolution?

5. The French Revolution is often characterized as the beginning of the end of the old regime in Europe, as well as a sign of things to come in the nineteenth and twentieth centuries. Comment on this statement using appropriate examples as necessary.

Chapter 20
THE AGE OF NAPOLEON AND THE TRIUMPH OF ROMANTICISM

Multiple-Choice
1. The Napoleonic Constitution of 1799
    (a) was outwardly dictatorial.
    (b) was modeled after that of the United States.
    (c) contained a suggestion of democratic principles and republican theories.
    (d) none of the above

2. With the Napoleonic Code of 1804
    (a) fathers had extensive control over their families.
    (b) the rights of employers were greater than the rights of workers
    (c) labor unions were forbidden.
    (d) all of the above

3. Napoleon's real reason for establishing the Bonapartist dynasty in 1804 was
    (a) the need to publicly demonstrate supremacy over the Church in France.
    (b) the need to demonstrate supremacy over the Pope.
    (c) that it represented a natural goal of his ambition.
    (d) necessary for him to get into college.

4. Which statement best describes Napoleon's treatment of the relatives he placed in control of European kingdoms?
    (a) He generally allowed them to make decisions.
    (b) He cared little for what they did.
    (c) He gave them orders and expected them to be carried out.
    (d) none of the above

5. Which of the following would not be associated with the reforms of the Napoleonic Code as it affected France and much of Europe?
    (a) Roman Catholic Church's monopoly on religion ended.
    (b) Feudal obligations of the peasants disappeared.
    (c) Class distinctions were reinforced.
    (d) The liberalizing ideas of the Enlightenment began to reach much of Europe.

6. Rebellion against French rule in Spain came from the
    (a) nobility and upper clergy.
    (b) peasants and monastic leaders.
    (c) upper classes.
    (d) peasants and the lower clergy.

7. Napoleon once explained to the Austrian foreign minister Metternich that
    (a) "I am an upstart soldier."
    (b) "All Europe owes me a debt of gratitude."
    (c) (c) "War is preferable to peace."
    (d) "I shall return."

8. Napoleon's final exile was to the island of
    (a) St. Helena.
    (b) Corsica.
    (c) Elba.
    (d) Sardinia.

9. Friedrich Schlegel's Lucinde (1799) shocked many contemporaries because
    (a) it openly discussed sexual activity.
    (b) it showed a woman in a heroic way.
    (c) it did not cater to existing prejudices against women.
    (d) all of the above

10. The idea that Christianity is the "religion of religion" is associated with
    (a) Immanuel Kant.
    (b) Friedrich Schleiermacher.
    (c) John Wesley.
    (d) François René de Chateaubriand.

True-False

_____1. With the complete support of the government at Paris, Napoleon negotiated the Treaty of Campo Formio (October 1797) that took the Austrian Empire out of the First Coalition.

_____2. In 1804, though overwhelmingly supported by the people of France, Napoleon still insisted on placing the imperial crown on his own head.

_____3. While negotiations for the Treaty of Tilsit were taking place, Russian Czar Alexander had to wait patiently on a riverbank.

_____4. The German political leaders von Stein and von Hardenburg generally supported democratic reform in Prussia.

_____5. Sir Arthur Wellesley commanded British forces during the Peninsular War in Spain.

_____6. The Grand Army of Napoleon, which invaded Russia in 1812, was composed of about 300,000 Frenchmen and the remaining half was drawn from all over Europe.

_____ 7. The combined armies of the other European states defeated Napoleon at Leipzig in 1813.

_____ 8. In Émile, Rousseau urged the importance of strict upbringing of children that they might later flourish as adults.

_____ 9. In his The Genius of Christianity, François Chateaubriand began his writing with this first statement, "My heart felt strangely warmed."

_____ 10. Methodism generally stressed the imperfectability of the Christian life.

Completion

1. After Napoleon's defeat of the Austrians in 1797, France's only enemy was _____ .

2. The execution of the _____ put an end to royalist plots against Napoleon's government.

3. Probably the battle at _____ against the combined forces of Russia and Austria was Napoleon's greatest victory.

4. One of the outcomes of the 1809 French victory at Wagram was Napoleon's marriage to _____ .

5. _____ was the French representative to the Congress of Vienna.

6. "Our imagination is God at work in the mind" would be associated with _____ and _____ , who were leading figures of English Romantic movement.

7. The most rebellious of the Romantic writers was _____ .

8. _____ is the story of a man who, weary of life, made a pact with the Devil.

9. _____ are known for their famous fairy tales.

10. _____ was the most important historical writer of the entire Romantic era.

Short Answer

1. Explain the rise of Napoleon Bonaparte. Can this be considered a classic example of man making history, or were conditions favorable to the emergence of a "Napoleon-like" leader?

2. How did France under Napoleon actually control Europe? Was there a common theme to all of Napoleon's actions during this era? Why were the European states for so long unable to organize against the French threat?

3. Discuss the circumstances that brought about the Congress of Vienna. What were the major successes and failures of the meeting? Are there any long-term, historical factors to be associated with the Congress of Vienna? If so, what are they?

4. Define Romanticism. What do you see as the overall impact of this concept on Western civilization?

Chapter 21
THE CONSERVATIVE ORDER AND THE CHALLENGES OF REFORM (1815–1832)

Multiple-Choice
1. The real goal of this era's political liberals was
    (a) mass democracy.
    (b) political reform based on property ownership.
    (c) free education for all.
    (d) the end of poverty.

2. _____ was an important complement to liberalism in this period.
    (a) Economic Liberalism
    (b) Nationalism
    (c) Christianity
    (d) Urbanization

3. _____ was not an English radical.
    (a) Edmund Burke
    (b) William Cobbett
    (c) John Cartwright
    (d) Henry Hunt

4. Alexander I's reign (1801–1825) can be considered as
    (a) liberal throughout
    (b) conservative throughout
    (c) initially liberal and later conservative
    (d) none of the above

5. The Concert of Europe was
    (a) a radical political party.
    (b) the dream child of the Russian Tsar.
    (c) a symphony orchestra.
    (d) none of the above

6. What became known as the Eastern Question in European affairs was actually a reflection of the
    (a) war for Greek independence.
    (b) weakness of the Ottoman Empire.
    (c) European fear of Russia.
    (d) Polish resistance to Russian reform programs there.

7. Early in the nineteenth century _____ assumed the role as a protector of Serbia.
   (a) Austria
   (b) England
   (c) France
   (d) Russia

8. The Decembrists in Russia wanted to achieve all of the following except
   (a) constitutional government.
   (b) election of Czars.
   (c) Constantine to be Czar.
   (d) abolition of serfdom.

9. The Four Ordinances issued by Charles X
   (a) restricted freedom of the press/
   (b) (b)restricted the franchise to only the wealthiest people in the country
   (c) brought a strong reaction throughout much of French society.
   (d) all of the above

10. The Great Reform Bill of 1832 finally passed because
    (a) of fears of mob violence.
    (b) new elections were held for the House of Commons.
    (c) the king threatened to alter the structure of the House of Lords.
    (d) of the Peterloo Massacre.

True-False

_____ 1. "Trouble-breeding and usually thought-obscuring terms," is a critical reference to the ideals of the Enlightenment.

_____ 2. The so-called Cato Street Conspiracy was aimed at the assassination of Britain's George III.

_____ 3. An important factor in repressive measures taken by Louis XVIII of France can be found in the 1820 murder of the Duke de Berri.

_____ 4. Czar Alexander I of Russia was considered the chief architect of the post-Vienna world through the first quarter of the nineteenth century.

_____ 5. Creole leaders in Latin America could be said to have developed a reform program based upon Enlightenment ideas and those associated with the American Revolution.

_____ 6. Mexico was the first area within Latin America to rise in revolution against Spain.

_____ 7. The statement, "There is no doubt that serfdom in its present form, is a flagrant evil which everyone realizes, yet to attempt to remedy it now would be, of course, an evil more disastrous," can be considered an indication of the difficulty of reform in Russia during the first half of the nineteenth century.

_____ 8. By the declaration of Nicholas I's Organic Statute, Poland became an integral part of the Russian empire.

_____ 9. The so-called July Monarchy was headed by Louis Philippe as King of the French.

_____ 10. In 1832, England's Great Reform Bill extended the electoral franchise to all males over the age of twenty-one.

Completion

1. It is clear today that a common _____ is required as a basic block for the establishment of a new nation.

2. Many of the ideas of nineteenth-century liberals can be attributed to the writers of the _____.

3. During this period German student associations were called _____.

4. _____ was the first king of France after the abdication of Napoleon.

5. The document which declared that stable governments could intervene in other countries troubled by revolution and disorder was the _____.

6. The hero of Chilean independence was _____.

7. The French city of _____ witnessed more than one serious workers' strike during the 1830s.

8. The first king of an independent Belgium was _____.

9. One of the most important articles of international relations until World War I had to do with the neutrality of _____.

10. The 1829 _____ Act passed by the British Parliament was directly related to the Irish Question.

Short Answer

1. What was it about the nature of German society that made the plight of liberals there different? Can you envision what the future direction of German liberalism would be later in the nineteenth century?

2. Why is the movement for independence in Haiti viewed as the exception when compared with similar revolts throughout Latin America in this era? Has this altered Haiti's development into our time? Comment on recent Haitian troubles in this regard.

3. In regard to the revolutionary movements in Latin America during this period review the motives and role played by Creole elites. Compare their position with that of the European liberal movements at that time. Support your answer fully.

4. Throughout the nineteenth century, Russia was considered as the most conservative, least reform-minded, anti-liberal state. In your opinion what were the major reasons for this position?

Chapter 22
ECONOMIC ADVANCE AND SOCIAL UNREST (1830–1850)

Multiple-Choice

1. Which of the following did not contribute to the industrial strength of Great Britain in the nineteenth century?
    - (a) Natural resources
    - (b) German technological advances
    - (c) adequate financial resources
    - (d) considerable mobility within society

2. The largest railroad network in Europe before 1850 could be found in
    - (a) England.
    - (b) France.
    - (c) Belgium.
    - (d) Germany.

3. Which of the following groups would not be considered a part of the early nineteenth-century labor force?
    - (a) Urban artisans and factory workers
    - (b) shopkeepers and inventors
    - (c) farm workers and countryside peddlers
    - (d) the working poor

4. Which of the following would not be considered part of the Chartist reform program?
    - (a) women's rights
    - (b) annual election of the House of Commons
    - (c) universal manhood suffrage
    - (d) salaries for Members of Parliament

5. Which of the following is the most correct statement about the process of industrialization?
    - (a) The newer and larger machines required more skilled laborers.
    - (b) The English Factory Act of 1833 had little effect.
    - (c) New modes of work were created for many young women.
    - (d) none of the above

6. Apparently, the real reason for the repeal of the British Corn Laws was
    - (a) both rich and poor wanted corn from American farms.
    - (b) the famine in Ireland.
    - (c) it would appease the radical wing of the Chartist movement.
    - (d) it would immediately reduce wages of factory workers.

7. Which of the following was not a major source of Karl Marx's ideas?
    (a) German Hegelianism
    (b) utopian socialism
    (c) French socialism
    (d) British economic theory.

8. Demands of French women's groups during the revolution of 1848 included all of the following except
    (a) religious freedom.
    (b) economic security.
    (c) educational opportunities.
    (d) the right to vote.

9. _____ led the Hungarian uprising against the Hapsburgs in 1848–1850.
    (a) Alphonse Lamartine
    (b) Friedrich Engels
    (c) Louis Blanc
    (d) Louis Kossuth

10. Whom of the following is not associated with the conservative reaction to the revolutions of 1848?
    (a) General Garibaldi
    (b) General Cavaignac
    (c) General Radetzky
    (d) General Windischgaetz

True-False

_____ 1. By the middle of the nineteenth century, England was the most populous country of Europe.

_____ 2. The most dramatic application of steam technology was in the growth of railroads in Europe.

_____ 3. Among the Chartist reforms were demands for salaries for elected members of the House of Commons.

_____ 4. Though there were many eighteenth-century textile related inventions, it was the mechanization of weaving that had the greatest effect on the methods of work.

_____ 5. The least likely early employment occupation for a young woman was domestic service.

_____ 6. One of the theories of a policed society is that the visibility of law enforcement personnel will, in itself, deter crime.

_____ 7. Unlike the system developed at New York's Auburn prison, the Philadelphia system called for the complete isolation of the prisoners from each other.

_____ 8. The major European utopian socialists expected their reforming ideas to prevail as a result of mass revolutions by the workers.

_____ 9. While no single condition could have caused the upheavals of 1848, widespread food shortages and unemployment are factors to be considered.

_____ 10. Feminist efforts in France during the mid-century revolutions there, led to near full acceptance of their agenda.

Completion

1. By the middle of the nineteenth century, half the population of _____ lived in an urban setting.

2. The most important spokesman for the Chartist Movement was _____ .

3. The now famous Essay on the Principal of Population, first appearing in 1798, was written by _____ .

4. _____ wrote short stories that helped popularize the new economic thoughts of the time.

5. The socialist experiment at New Harmony, Indiana (U.S.A.) was established by _____ .

6. The author of the work *What Is Property?* was the anarchist _____ .

7. Though the son of a middle-class factory owner, _____ was a fellow revolutionary of Karl Marx.

8. For _____ the victory of the proletariat over the bourgeoisie represented the culmination of human history.

9. The state of _____ was viewed by many Italians as the one capable of ridding Italy of Austrian domination.

10. The Frankfurt Parliament made little headway on the issue of German _____ .

Short Answer

1. Within a general discussion of the rise of industrialization in Europe, what do the authors mean by the statement, "Industrialism had begun to grow on itself"?

2. Discuss the changing nature of the family in the first half of the nineteenth century. Note the role of industrialization in the lives of men, women, and children. Support your ideas fully.

3. Compare and contrast the utopian socialist ideas of Saint-Simon, Owen, and Fourier.

4. Define Marxism. Realistically what were Marx's goals within the framework of his idea of the proletarian revolution?

5. Briefly review the revolutionary events of 1848 in France, Italy, Austria, and Germany. How is it that Russia and Great Britain were untouched by the contagion of revolution in this period? After achieving some initial successes, most of the revolutionary movements of 1848 failed. Why?

Chapter 23
THE AGE OF NATION-STATES

Multiple-Choice

1. Which is the most accurate statement concerning the Crimean War?
    (a) Both sides had well-equipped armies.
    (b) After the war instability prevailed in Europe for several decades.
    (c) The Concert of Europe ended.
    (d) There was no formal peace treaty to end the war.

2. The person most responsible for the final unification of Italy in 1861 was
    (a) Niccolò Machiavelli.
    (b) Guiseppe Garibaldi.
    (c) Camillo Cavour.
    (d) Felice Orsini.

3. During the 1860s, the Papal States were guarded by the troops of
    (a) Piedmont.
    (b) Austria.
    (c) France.
    (d) Prussia.

4. The correct chronological order of Bismarck's moves leading to the unification of Germany was in victories against
    (a) Denmark, Austria, France.
    (b) Austria, Denmark, France.
    (c) France, Denmark, Austria.
    (d) France, Austria, Denmark.

5. The immediate origins of the Franco-Prussian War lie in troubles within the monarchy of
    (a) Prussia.
    (b) France.
    (c) Spain.
    (d) Denmark.

6. Which of the following occurred the earliest?
    (a) the secret conference at Plombières
    (b) the death of Cavour
    (c) the formation of the North German Confederation
    (d) the Treaty of Frankfurt

7. A politician who acquired considerable prestige in France's turbulent politics of the 1880s and who might have led a successful coup against the Third Republic was
    (a) Adolphe Thiers.
    (b) Georges Boulanger.
    (c) Marshal MacMahon.
    (d) Leon Gambetta.

8. Before the 1860s, the usual period of service for Russian military recruits was
    (a) 6 months.
    (b) 5 years.
    (c) 10 years.
    (d) 25 years.

9. The Russian monarch Alexander III
    (a) freed the serfs.
    (b) was a thoroughgoing reformer.
    (c) was the grandfather of Nicholas II.
    (d) was autocratic and repressive.

10. Two of the most important Prime Ministers of England during the 1860s and 1870s were
    (a) Peel and Derby.
    (b) Disraeli and Gladstone.
    (c) Palmerston and Aberdeen.
    (d) Cross and Russell.

True-False

_____1. In the pursuit of Italian unification Count Cavour once declared that, "nationality is the role assigned by God to a people in the work of humanity. It is its mission, its task on earth, to the end that God's thought may be realized in the world."

_____2. The Treaty of Villafranca concluded the process of Italian unification.

_____3. When his brother Frederick William IV was judged insane, William I effectively became the ruler of Prussia.

_____4. Otto von Bismarck's famous "Blood and Iron" speech noted that the liberal-sponsored efforts at reform fostered during the 1848–1849 period had failed.

_____5. In the midst of the Franco-Prussian War when Paris was besieged by the German army, Marseille became the temporary capital of France.

_____6. One of the announced goals of the Paris Commune was "free love."

_____ 7. In 1871, the Bourbon claimant to the throne refused to accept the revolutionary flag of France and was therefore bypassed, in favor of the formation of the Third French Republic.

_____ 8. "A standing army of soldiers, a kneeling army of priests, and a crawling army of informers," was a reference to the Austrian Empire.

_____ 9. In the last quarter of the last century, territorial integrity became the single most important factor in defining a nation.

_____ 10. The Education Act of 1870 and the Ballot Act of 1872 should each be considered the outcome of British conservative politics.

Completion

1. _____ was the one nation outside of Piedmont that was particularly supportive of the movement for Italian unification.

2. A function of mid-century Italian politics, the policy of _____ in bribery and corruption.

3. Between 1861 and 1867 _____ led a French-supported expedition against Mexico.

4. One of the most dramatic affairs of French life in the 1890s revolved around an army officer named _____ .

5. J'accuse was written by _____ .

6. _____ was the name given to the document that created the so-called Dual Monarchy.

7. The Russian nobility had a large role in affairs of local governance through the system of provincial councils known as _____ .

8. A revolutionary movement supported by many students and intellectuals in Russia was known as _____ .

9. "What then occurred surprised everyone," is a reference to the circumstances surrounding the passage of the _____ .

10. The leader of the movement for Irish Home Rule was _____ .

Short Answer

1. Examine the respective roles of the participants and neutrals in the Crimean War. Which countries gained/lost by their actions in the conflict? Explain your answer fully.

2. Compare and contrast the processes involved in the unification of Italy with those involved in the unification of Germany.

3. How would you characterize the political climate in France from the time of that nation's defeat in 1871 until the end of the nineteenth century? Be sure to discuss in detail how the Dreyfus Affair played a major role at this time.

4. Discuss what you consider to be the basic weakness of the Austrian Empire during Francis Joseph's reign.

5. Throughout much of the nineteenth century, why did England remain the most liberally progressive of the European states?

Chapter 24
THE BUILDING OF EUROPEAN SUPREMACY: SOCIETY AND POLITICS TO WORLD WAR I

Multiple-Choice

1. Between 1860 and 1914
    (a) Europe's financial and industrial supremacy emerged.
    (b) socialism became an influential part of European political life.
    (c) the modern basis of the consumer economy emerged in Europe.
    (d) all of the above

2. By 1910 the population of Europe reached nearly
    (a) 600 million.
    (b) 450 million.
    (c) 300 million.
    (d) 150 million.

3. Which of the following is the most accurate statement about the development of European cities in the second half of the nineteenth century?
    (a) The central portions of many major cities were redesigned.
    (b) The middle classes began to look for housing outside of city centers.
    (c) Commercialization of city centers took place.
    (d) all of the above

4. Important new medical practices became a part of European life in this era because of the research of all of the following, except
    (a) Georges Haussmann in France.
    (b) Robert Koch in Germany.
    (c) Joseph Lister in Britain.
    (d) Louis Pasteur in France.

5. The most advanced women's movement in Europe could be found in
    (a) The Austro-Hungarian Empire.
    (b) Great Britain.
    (c) France.
    (d) the Netherlands.

6. Which of the following is the most correct statement about trades unions by 1900?
    (a) They were completely suppressed in Germany.
    (b) Most members were unskilled laborers.
    (c) They were legalized in Germany, England, and France.
    (d) Only Great Britain permitted their existence.

7. The collapse of the First International can be attributed to
    (a) the success of British unionism.
    (b) growth and influence of other socialist organizations.
    (c) events surrounding the Paris Commune.
    (d) all of the above

8. The type of socialism that aimed at gradual and peaceful change within the existing sociopolitical framework was known as
    (a) trade unionism.
    (b) Marxism.
    (c) Fabianism.
    (d) syndicalism.

9. Bismarck's response to the efforts of the German socialists was
    (a) a repression of the socialist parties.
    (b) health insurance.
    (c) government-sponsored social welfare programs.
    (d) all of the above

10. The most notable Russian Marxist of the nineteenth century was
    (a) Vladimir Ulyanov.
    (b) Gregory Plekhanov.
    (c) Sergei Witt.
    (d) P. A. Stolypin.

True-False

_____ 1. The out-migration of Europeans to the United States, Canada, South Africa, and Argentina had the effect of relieving social pressures on the Continent.

_____ 2. Concern for urban riots was among the factors that prompted Louis Napoleon's rebuilding of the city of Paris.

_____ 3. In the last half of the nineteenth century it became clear that new urban water and sewer systems would achieve considerable health benefits for the entire population.

_____ 4. Among the female population at this time, women who did not marry probably had the best time of it.

_____ 5. Too many women migrating to the cities caused the growth of prostitution.

_____ 6. Pogroms protected Jews from violence in Russia.

_____ 7. The membership of the First International included Polish nationalists, socialists, political radicals, and even anarchists.

_____ 8. For participating in a plot against Czar Alexander III, Lenin's older brother was executed in 1887.

_____ 9. "Bloody Sunday" was a 1905 event in which several thousand Russian workers and poor successfully attacked the Czar's Winter Palace in Saint Petersburg.

_____ 10. The authors of the text assert that during the latter part of the nineteenth century Europe experienced the emergence of socialism, labor unions, contradictory life-styles, and growing demands of women in politics.

Completion

1. The growth of the chemical industry at the end of the nineteenth century was especially fostered by this nation: _____ .

2. The single most important aspect of the later industrial revolution was in the use of _____ for production.

3. After 1850, the _____ became the arbiter of consumer taste and defender of the status quo.

4. By 1910, the city with the largest population in Europe was _____ .

5. _____ was a phrase used to depict instances of cooperation between French socialists and the government.

6. _____ was the author of Evolutionary Socialism (1899).

7. The person who led Russia into the industrial age was _____ .

8. In Russia the more prosperous peasant farmers were known as _____ .

9. Lenin's group within the Russian Social Democratic Party was known as the _____ .

10. Instrumental in causing serious unrest in Russia in 1905 was that country's defeat by _____ .

Short Answer

1. Explain in detail the differences between the First and Second Industrial Revolutions.

2. Describe the position of women within the middle-class household and within society generally at the end of the nineteenth century.

3. Describe in detail the key elements of the feminist movement at the end of the nineteenth and into the early part of the twentieth century. Be sure to discuss the leading personalities of the movement and list their most important goals.

4. Compare and contrast any three of the non-Russian socialist theories of this era.

5. As exemplified in his pamphlet What Is to Be Done?, what were Lenin's ideas and how were they different from the ideas of others in the Russian Social Democratic party?

Chapter 25
THE BIRTH OF MODERN EUROPEAN THOUGHT

Multiple-Choice

1. By the turn of the century which of the following European states had the highest literacy rate?
    - (a) Spain
    - (b) Austria-Hungary
    - (c) Belgium
    - (d) d) Italy

2. Three stages of human development—theological, metaphysical, and positivist stem from the thought of
    - (a) Émile Durkheim.
    - (b) Auguste Comte.
    - (c) Thomas Henry Huxley.
    - (d) Claude Bernard.

3. In his *Life of Jesus*, _____ cast doubt on the origins of Christianity.
    - (a) Julius Wellhausen
    - (b) David Friederich Strauss
    - (c) William Robertson Smith
    - (d) Ernst Renan

4. The dogma of the infallibility of the pope in matters of faith and morals stems from the
    - (a) concept of Catholic Modernism.
    - (b) First Vatican Council.
    - (c) *Rerum Novarum*.
    - (d) Syllabus of Errors.

5. Pope Leo XIII's encyclical *Rerum Novarum* supported all of the following except
    - (a) just wages.
    - (b) private property.
    - (c) socialism.
    - (d) religious education.

6. _____ is considered to have discovered radium.
    - (a) Marie Curie
    - (b) Werner Heisenberg
    - (c) Leo Tolstoy
    - (d) Max Planck

7. The word "overman" is most clearly associated with the thinking of
    (a) Friedrich Nietzsche.
    (b) Pope Pius XI.
    (c) George Gissing.
    (d) Émile Zola.

8. "The dream is the fulfillment of a wish" is a phrase best associated with
    (a) Henry Bergson.
    (b) Max Planck.
    (c) Sigmund Freud.
    (d) Leo Tolstoy.

9. Which of the following names would not be considered as that of an anti-Semitic writer or politician?
    (a) Theodor Herzl
    (b) Adolf Stoecker
    (c) Karl Leugar
    (d) Houston S. Chamberlain

10. With A Room of One's Own Virginia Woolf opened
    (a) a new discussion of sexual morality.
    (b) the whole question of gender definition.
    (c) an assault against the male dominated literary world.
    (d) demands for living space for single women.

True-False

_____1. Intellectual life in the last half of the nineteenth century was altered by the existence of a mass reading audience.

_____2. In 1830 Charles Lyell established the basis of the modern theory of chemical composition.

_____3. The replacement of the Falloux Law of 1850 with the so-called Ferry Laws effectively removed religious education from the public schools of France.

_____4. At the turn of the century both Max Planck and Albert Einstein were challenging the conventional theories of physics.

_____5. In his Androcles and the Lion George Bernard Shaw gave high praise to Christianity's support of high ethical principles throughout the ages.

_____6. Friedrich Nietzsche, whose first important philosophical work was titled *The Birth of Tragedy*, was actually trained in the study of ancient literary texts.

_____ 7. The Austrian physician Sigmund Freud believed that the innocence of childhood, particularly in regard to sexual things, should be preserved with great care until at least puberty.

_____ 8. The publication of Carl Jung's *Modern Man in Search of a Soul* in 1933, completely reversed Freud's views on dreams.

_____ 9. Arthur de Gobineau's theories of racial determinism expressed in his Essay on the Inequality of the Human Races noted that the process of degeneration would end within a century.

_____ 10. The idea that the Jewish question is not a social or religious, but international problem, is associated with Theodor Herzl.

Completion

1. _____ was the scientist who first began to unravel the mystery of heredity.

2. The terms "evolutionary ethics" and "social Darwinism" are associated with the works of _____ .

3. "War and courage have accomplished more great things than love of neighbor" is a phrase associated with the writings of _____ .

4. Pope Pius IX's issuance of the _____ was a clear sign of the Church's antiliberal stance.

5. _____ is often considered the first genuinely realistic novel.

6. In the play _____ George Bernard Shaw explored the matter of prostitution.

7. _____ wrote To the Lighthouse.

8. _____ was a student of Freud who later could not accept the idea that sex played the prime role in the formation of the human personality.

9. The Protestant Ethic and the Spirit of Capitalism was written by _____ .

10. Late in the nineteenth century _____ attitudes were fostered through a variety of factors such as pressures created by change, the insecurities of the new middle classes, and Jewish domination of money and banking interests.

Short Answer

1. Discuss several factors that gave rise to increased literacy in Europe by the end of the nineteenth century. Why was the increase in literacy so important to the intellectual and scientific developments of the era?

2. Examine the broad-based attacks upon the Christian churches in the late nineteenth century. What were the origins of these challenges to religious authority? What were the results?

3. Describe the views of the German writer Friedrich Nietzsche. Are his views relevant or irrelevant today?

4. How do you assess the impact of the works of Sigmund Freud? What were the chief positions taken in his pioneering studies?

5. A. Discuss the foundations of the revival of anti-Semitism in Europe at the turn of the century. What conditions, if any, supported the movements against the Jews?
   B. Discuss the foundations of the Feminist movement at the turn of the century. Why was there an insistence upon defining gender roles?

Chapter 26
IMPERIALISM, ALLIANCES, AND WAR

Multiple-Choice
1. Imperialism may have been profitable for some European states, but for these two states it clearly was a losing proposition
    (a) France and Russia.
    (b) Germany and Italy.
    (c) Italy and Great Britain.
    (d) Germany and Turkey.

2. Which of the following areas was the least vulnerable to European expansion at the end of the nineteenth-century?
    (a) China
    (b) South America
    (c) Ottoman Empire
    (d) Africa

3. Which of the following is not a result of the Congress of Berlin of 1878?
    (a) Austria-Hungary gained the provinces of Bosnia and Herzegovina.
    (b) The Three Emperors' League was dead.
    (c) Bulgaria was reduced in size.
    (d) All of these were results of the meeting.

4. The three states of the Triple Alliance were
    (a) Germany, Russia, and Austria-Hungary.
    (b) Great Britain, France, and Russia.
    (c) Germany, Austria-Hungary, and Italy.
    (d) Russia, France, and Serbia.

5. The three states of the Triple Entente were
    (a) Germany, Russia, and Austria-Hungary.
    (b) Great Britain, France, and Russia.
    (c) Germany, Austria-Hungary, and Italy.
    (d) Russia, France, and Serbia.

6. Of all of the major powers involved, which of the two appear to have been most responsible for the outbreak of the World War I?
    (a) Great Britain and France
    (b) Germany and Great Britain
    (c) Russia and Austria-Hungary
    (d) Germany and Austria

7. Throughout the war the most effective basic new weapon was the
    (a) machine gun,.
    (b) tank.
    (c) submarine.
    (d) airplane.

8. Lenin and the Bolsheviks signed the Treaty of Brest-Litovsk in 1918 because
    (a) Russia was not able to carry on the war effort.
    (b) Lenin's government needed time to impose its will on the Russian people.
    (c) Lenin believed that communism would soon sweep through the warring states of Europe.
    (d) all of the above

9. One of the factors that appeared to hasten the peacemakers at Paris to conclude the Treaty of Versailles was
    (a) the threat of a renewed war with Germany.
    (b) the spread of Russian-inspired Bolshevism.
    (c) the near collapse of France.
    (d) President Wilson's political problems at home.

10. With regard to eastern Europe the settlements of the Paris Peace Conference included all of the following except
    (a) Bulgaria was enlarged from territory of Greece and Yugoslavia.
    (b) the complete disappearance of the Austro-Hungarian Empire.
    (c) Finland, Estonia, Latvia, and Lithuania became independent states.
    (d) the Magyars were left in control of the new Hungarian state.

True-False

_____ 1. A novel aspect of the so-called New Imperialism was the efforts of the imperial power to integrate the native inhabitants into the managerial structure of the colony.

_____ 2. During this period the English statesman Joseph Chamberlain advanced the idea of overseas empires serving as a source of profit that could be utilized to finance domestic reform and welfare programs in the home country.

_____ 3. The effort to keep France isolated in Europe was a cornerstone of Bismarck's policy.

_____ 4. The First Moroccan Crisis was temporarily resolved at a 1906 international meeting held at Algeciras, Spain.

_____ 5. An integral part of the Second Moroccan Crisis was the British assumption that Germany was moving to establish a naval base there.

_____ 6. When he was murdered in Sarajevo, Archduke Francis Ferdinand was considered one of the most popular figures in the Austro-Hungarian monarchy.

_____ 7. At the time of the outbreak of World War I the mobilization of the armed forces of any country was interpreted as a bluff and not to be taken seriously.

_____ 8. Italy was lured into World War I against Germany and Austria-Hungary as a result of territorial promises made by the Western Allies.

_____ 9. Russian Mensheviks believed, like Karl Marx, that a proletarian revolution could occur only after the bourgeois stage of development.

_____ 10. At the end of World War I a right-wing group emerged under the name of "Spartacus" and challenged the newly established government of Germany.

Completion

1. The English economist _____ is one of the first to give an economic interpretation to imperialism in this era.

2. The phrase, "My map of Africa lies in Europe," is associated with this statesman: _____ .

3. The so-called _____ brought the empires of Germany, Russia, and Austria-Hungary together in 1873.

4. _____ was the country that gained the least from the 1878 Congress of Berlin.

5. The expression, "What kind of jackass will dare to be Bismarck's successor?" is associated with _____ .

6. The architect of the new German navy was _____ .

7. It can be said that Britain's isolation ended with her treaty with _____ .

8. "They shall not pass," is a slogan associated with the great battle of _____ .

9. _____ and _____ were nations both excluded from the newly formed League of Nations.

10. In the last analysis, it was _____ which would have to defend the arrangements made at the Paris Peace Conference.

Short Answer

1. Discuss several of the causes of the so-called "New Imperialism." In your opinion which countries in their colonial efforts gained an advantage and which countries gained little or nothing for their efforts?

2. Give an overall year-by-year review of the important military strategies and events of World War I.

3. Describe the economic and political realities in Russia during World War I. In your opinion should Lenin and the Bolsheviks have been surprised at their seemingly sudden success? Explain your answer fully.

4. In an analysis of the results of the Versailles settlement list what can be considered as specific successes and failures of the Paris Peace Conference of 1919. Briefly explain each one.

5. Compare and contrast the conditions of European politics and society that existed at the time of the Congress of Vienna (1815) with those existing at the time of the Paris Peace Conference (1919).

Chapter 27
POLITICAL EXPERIMENTS OF THE 1920S

Multiple-Choice

1. Attempts to revise the Treaty of Versailles normally stemmed from such problems as
    (a) reparations questions.
    (b) inadequate enforcement of the Treaty.
    (c) demands for greater self-determination.
    (d) all of the above

2. One of the most significant social changes brought on by the war was the elevated position of particularly
    (a) the elderly.
    (b) disabled veterans.
    (c) labor unions.
    (d) all of the above

3. Which of the following was not listed among Lenin's "commanding heights"?
    (a) heavy industry
    (b) agriculture
    (c) banking
    (d) international commerce

4. Stalin's strength seems to have been derived from the fact that he was
    (a) a master of administrative methods.
    (b) an excellent writer.
    (c) a gifted speaker.
    (d) witty and flashy.

5. Which of the following is the most correct statement about Mussolini?
    (a) He was always a nationalist.
    (b) He was always a socialist.
    (c) He originally was a socialist and became a nationalist during World War I.
    (d) He always put the nation before himself.

6. Secret military connections were initiated between Germany and the Soviet Union as a result of the
    (a) Treaty of Rapallo.
    (b) Kellogg-Briand Pact
    (c) Locarno Agreements.
    (d) Rentenmark.

7. In 1918 the British electorate included
    (a) men aged twenty-one and women aged twenty-five.
    (b) only men.
    (c) men aged twenty-one and women aged thirty.
    (d) men and women aged twenty-one.

8. In the 1920s the Irish Civil War lingered over the issue of
    (a) the six counties of Ulster.
    (b) the oath of allegiance to the monarchy.
    (c) Protestants within the Irish Free State.
    (d) neutrality in world affairs.

9. Article 48 of the Weimar Republic's Constitution
    (a) gave the Reichstag veto power over the President.
    (b) established the basis for proportional representation in the Reichstag.
    (c) severely curtailed presidential authority.
    (d) gave greater power to the president in times of emergency.

10. The original appeal of the Nazi party appears to have been to
    (a) the wealthy.
    (b) war veterans.
    (c) the communists.
    (d) farmers and laborers.

True-False

_____1. In the spirit of political experimentation after the First World War, most countries attempted several democratic forms of government before turning to authoritarianism.

_____2. Compared to the other ideologies of this era Russian communists believed that Marxism-Leninism could be established throughout the world.

_____3. After the stringent economics policies of "War Communism" Lenin somewhat reversed his position with his sponsorship of the New Economic Policy.

_____4. Josef Stalin advocated the policy of "socialism in one country."

_____5. During the 1920s French politicians often campaigned on the slogan that France should be a land fit for heroes to live in.

_____6. Bela Kun, Miklos Horthy, Julius Gombos and Kurt von Schuschnigg are all associated with the turbulent politics of Hungary during the post-war era.

_____7. The actual reparations "bill" presented to Germany by the Allies in 1921 amounted to 132 million gold marks.

_____ 8. By 1922 Hitler and the Nazi's were defining socialism along traditional German ideological lines.

_____ 9. The election of Paul von Hindenburg to the presidency in 1925 suggests an accommodation of conservative elements to the reality of the Weimar Republic.

_____ 10. The overall results of the many political experiments of the 1920s should be characterized as mixed at best.

Completion
1. In the era before World War II, the idea of permanent communist revolution throughout the world would be associated with the name _____ .

2. The general term of _____ is often used to describe the right-wing dictatorships that came into being before World War II.

3. _____ was the king of Italy from 1900 to 1946.

4. A sensational example of Mussolini's willingness to use force and violence appears in the murder of _____ .

5. Mussolini's settlement with the Roman Catholic Church in 1929 was known as the _____ .

6. The General Strike of 1926 in Great Britain began when _____ went out on strike.

7. During World War I the only national group to rise violently against a government was the _____ .

8. The only government carved out of the collapsed Austro-Hungarian Empire to avoid a form of authoritarian government after World War I was _____ .

9. During the Ruhr crisis of 1923 the American dollar was worth _____ German marks.

10. As a result of the agreements at _____ a new atmosphere of hope and optimism appeared throughout Europe.

Short Answer

1. The struggle for power between Leon Trotsky and Josef Stalin has long been a subject for study by students of Communist Russia. What were the chief issues that divided these two men? Can you envision other factors that may have entered into the struggle?

2. Describe the manner of the Fascist takeover in Italy in 1922. What were the historic forces operating that brought Mussolini to power? How would you assess Mussolini's abilities as a politician?

3. With attention to specific problems, compare and contrast the postwar situation in Great Britain and in France.

4. Describe the inter-war development of Poland, Hungary, Czechoslovakia (now the Czech Republic and Slovakia), and Yugoslavia (Kingdom of Serbs, Croats and Slovenes)?

5. Discuss the events that helped shape Nazi power in Germany. What was the political climate in Germany and how did it contribute to Hitler's rise to power?

Chapter 28
EUROPE AND THE GREAT DEPRESSION OF THE 1930S

Multiple-Choice
1. The world commodity market of the 1930s saw
    (a) food production surpass demand.
    (b) government-accumulated reserves at record levels.
    (c) the price of food stuffs drop severely.
    (d) all of the above

2. _____ was not among the British Prime Ministers that had to come to grips with the economic problems stemming from the Great Depression.
    (a) Stanley Baldwin
    (b) Winston Churchill
    (c) Neville Chamberlain
    (d) Ramsay MacDonald

3. Right-wing groups in France such as the Action Française and the Croix de Feu were opposed to all of the following except
    (a) military rule.
    (b) socialism
    (c) communism.
    (d) parliamentary rule.

4. The country that actually suffered from the greatest unemployment problem in the late 1920s and the early 1930s was
    (a) Germany.
    (b) Italy.
    (c) France.
    (d) Great Britain.

5. By the 1930s support for the Nazi party within Germany came from all of the following except
    (a) the young.
    (b) farmers.
    (c) most intellectuals.
    (d) war veterans.

6. As far as it is known the formal decision to exterminate European Jews occurred in
    (a) 1933.
    (b) 1935.
    (c) 1942.
    (d) 1944.

7. Which of the following was not a part of Mussolini's economic program?
   (a) importation of foreign grain supplies
   (b) vast public works programs
   (c) protective tariffs
   (d) subsidies to industries

8. Between the years 1928 and 1940 Soviet industrial growth appears to have been near
   (a) 100 percent.
   (b) 400 percent.
   (c) 200 percent.
   (d) 50 percent.

9. "I have seen the future and it works," is a phrase ascribed to
   (a) Beatrice Webb.
   (b) Franklin Roosevelt.
   (c) Joseph Stalin.
   (d) Lincoln Steffens.

10. Which of the following events occurred first?
    (a) Hindenburg defeats Hitler for the presidency of Germany.
    (b) New York stock market collapses.
    (c) Sergei Kirov is assassinated.
    (d) Reichstag fire

True-False

_____1. Disruption in the world marketplace and the financial crisis caused by World War I led to the Great Depression.

_____2. In the years immediately after the war it was the United States that insisted upon repayment of allied war debts.

_____3. The idea of increasing government spending to offset the effects of the Depression is normally associated with British Prime Minister Ramsay MacDonald.

_____4. Sir Oswald Mosley's British Union of Fascists lost popularity in the mid 1930s as a result of his growing anti-Semitism.

_____5. Léon Blum's leadership of the French Popular Front aimed at establishing a socialist and democratic government.

_____6. In the 1932 Reichstag elections the Nazi party gained a clear parliamentary majority.

_____7. Anti-Semitism became a key element of the Nazi program in Germany only after Hitler gained power in 1933.

_____ 8. Lenin's New Economic Policy firmly established the economic program of communism in the Soviet Union.

_____ 9. The State Planning Commission (Gosplan) had the overall responsibility for industrial planning in the Soviet Union.

_____ 10. The best estimate for the number of people executed and imprisoned as a result of Stalin's purges is in the thousands.

Completion

1. The 1931 moratorium on all international debt was initiated by the American President _____ .

2. _____ wrote the General Theory of Employment Interest and Money.

3. In 1931 a British political coalition of labor, conservative, and liberal ministers formed the so-called _____ .

4. The _____ is a name given to the small group of advisers to Weimar President Hindenburg.

5. The incident of the _____ allowed Hitler to invoke Article 48 of the Constitution that would not be revoked until the end of World War II.

6. As a result of the death of _____, Hitler was able to combine the offices of chancellor and president into one.

7. By 1936 _____ was in charge of all police functions in Germany.

8. _____ were the 1935 series of laws passed against German Jews and their institutions.

9. _____ was the country invaded by Italy in 1935.

10. _____ is the word used to describe the agricultural reorganization of Russia under Stalin.

Short Answer

1. Describe the politics surrounding and the reform policies of Leon Blum and the Popular Front in France.

2. In an examination of German political maneuvering between 1930 and Hitler's appointment as Chancellor in 1933, what factors, beyond the clearly economic, seem to have undermined the Weimar Republic?

3. Using both Italian and German examples describe the economic system of fascism or corporatism. Generally, what was the fascist view of private property and of capital?

4. Describe the causes, aims, and effects of the Stalinist purges.

5. In your opinion why were the ruthless policies of the dictatorships of the 1930s possible?

Chapter 29
WORLD WAR II

Multiple-Choice

1. Which of the following represents the best explanation for the 1935 Italian invasion of Ethiopia?
    (a) economic conditions in Italy
    (b) the need to avenge the Italian defeat there in 1896
    (c) the desire to restore the glory of ancient Rome
    (d) all of the above

2. The establishment of the Spanish Republic in 1931 brought to power a government that supported
    (a) the Catholic Church
    (b) separatists and radicals
    (c) large landowners
    (d) none of the above

3. "I have no more territorial demands to make in Europe," is a statement by
    (a) Benito Mussolini.
    (b) Neville Chamberlain.
    (c) Konrad Henlein.
    (d) Adolf Hitler.

4. _____ contributed to Winston Churchill's success as a British leader.
    (a) His ability as a writer and speaker
    (b) His sense of history
    (c) His attitude toward British nationalism
    (d) all of the above

5. German racial policies were never really applied in
    (a) Norway.
    (b) Russia.
    (c) Poland.
    (d) the Slavic countries in general.

6. _____ would be considered along with Nazi Germany as unmatched in the committing of atrocities.
    (a) Italy
    (b) Soviet Union
    (c) Hungary
    (d) Romania

7. The 1945 "Battle of the Bulge" had the effect of showing that
    (a) Germany would soon lose the war.
    (b) years of tough fighting might possibly lie ahead.
    (c) Japan was finished.
    (d) American soldiers were no match for the Germans.

8. Which of the following statements best describes the reasons behind the decision to use the atomic bomb?
    (a) It was unnecessary to win the war, but it would teach the yellow races a lesson.
    (b) The use of the bomb by the United States would make the Russians more cooperative after the war
    (c) It was a way to end the war and save American lives.
    (d) The decision was not thought out at all.

9. During World War II German women were
    (a) portrayed as docile helpmates
    (b) forbidden to have sexual relations with non-Germans
    (c) not allowed to work in muntions factories
    (d) only permitted agriculturally related jobs.

10. As Woodrow Wilson was in an earlier era, President Franklin Roosevelt was
(a) suspicious of British motives.
(b) to place great faith in an international organization
(c) willing to make considerable compromises
(d) all of the above

True-False

_____1. Falangists were members of the pro-fascist parties opposing the Spanish Popular Front government in the Civil War there.

_____2. After signing the Munich agreements in September 1938, Hitler believed that it was "peace for our time."

_____3. One of the reasons behind the Nazi-Soviet Pact, secretly aimed at the division of Poland, was Stalin's distrust of the English and French after not being consulted over the partition of Czechoslovakia the previous year.

_____4. The French government that accepted defeat at the hands of the Germans ironically was led by a former World War I military hero.

_____5. Fighting in North Africa against both the British and the Americans earned German General Erwin Rommel the accolade of "The Desert Fox."

_____6. In late 1941 General Tojo led the Japanese militarists toward war with the United States.

_____ 7. Near the end of the war the determination of the Japanese to fight to the bitter end was evidenced by the suicide attacks of kamikaze planes.

_____ 8. That Japan could keep Hirohito as emperor was the only condition under which Japan surrendered to the United States on September 2, 1945.

_____ 9. In general, Vichy, France tended toward liberal excesses.

_____ 10. It's That Man Again was the name applied to Prime Minister Winston Churchill's broadcasts to the British people throughout World War II.

Completion

1. Nazi expansionist policies required the conquest of _____ and the _____ .

2. Haunted by the _____ of the last war, neither Great Britain nor France was willing to respond to Hitler's earlier provocations.

3. In 1936 General _____ led the revolt against the Spanish Popular Front.

4. In the late 1930's many of Adolf Hitler's gains came as a result of the British-French policy of _____ .

5. Within Nazi Germany's racial theory the Slavic peoples were considered as beasts or subhuman creatures known as _____ .

6. The German word _____ means "free of Jews."

7. The first reversal of Axis progress in World War II came with the American naval victory in the battle of the _____ .

8. The turning point of the Russian campaign came with the battle of _____ during the winter of 1942–1943.

9. The first meeting of the wartime allies (Churchill, Roosevelt, and Stalin) took place in _____ .

10. _____ was the only leader of the three major victorious powers who could attend both the Yalta and Potsdam Conferences.

Short Answer

1. Discuss the Munich Agreement of 1938. Outline the position of the states directly involved. Does this settlement contain any lessons for the contemporary world?

2. Discuss the questions surrounding high-altitude bombing during World War II. What were the primary and secondary targets? Was this method effective? Do the lessons learned in precision bombing during World War II have any effect on us today?

3. Suppose that the Nazis had not adopted the racial policies that they did. In your opinion, would the outcome of World War II have been any different? If the outcome had been the same, how might historians have come to judge the rise and fall of Adolf Hitler?

4. Considering the respective backgrounds of World War I and World War II, compare and contrast the founding of the League of Nations with the founding of the United Nations.

5. Discuss Stalin's policies and leadership throughout this period. In your opinion was Russia's position respective to the rise of Nazism equally responsible for the war?

Chapter 30
THE COLD WAR ERA AND THE EMERGENCE OF THE NEW EUROPE

Multiple-Choice

1. The Marshall Plan can be considered
    (a) a complete failure.
    (b) only moderately successful.
    (c) a great success.
    (d) neither a success nor failure.

2. Which is the correct post-World War II order for these presidents of the United States?
    (a) Ford, Carter, Nixon, Reagan, Bush
    (b) Eisenhower, Kennedy, Johnson, Ford, Carter
    (c) Truman, Eisenhower, Kennedy, Ford, Reagan
    (d) Johnson, Kennedy, Nixon, Ford, Reagan

3. Which is the correct post-World War II order for these leaders of the Soviet Union?
    (a) Andropov, Khrushchev, Brezhnev, Gorbachev
    (b) Stalin, Khrushchev, Yeltsin, Gorbachev
    (c) Chemenko, Khrushchev, Brezhnev, Andropov
    (d) none of the above

4. Russian Premier Khrushchev's abrupt ending of the 1960 Summit Conference at Paris was caused mainly by
    (a) an unsatisfactory settlement of the Berlin issue.
    (b) the Cuban Missile Crisis.
    (c) the U-2 incident.
    (d) his demand for President Eisenhower's resignation.

5. The "most dangerous days" of the Cold War thus far are usually associated with the
    (a) Korean War
    (b) construction of the Berlin Wall
    (c) Cuban Missile Crisis
    (d) American intervention in Vietnam.

6. _____ is considered to have been the most powerful Russian leader since Stalin's era.
    (a) Alexei Kosygin
    (b) Nikita Khrushchev
    (c) Leonid Brezhnev
    (d) Lavrenti Beria

7. The strike in _____ was the catalyst for change in Poland, and led to a change in political leadership.
    (a) Leningrad
    (b) Warsaw
    (c) St. Petersburg
    (d) Gdansk

8. During his presidency, Reagan intensified Cold War rhetoric, describing the Soviet Union as
    (a) an "evil empire".
    (b) a "most dangerous place".
    (c) "hell on earth".
    (d) none of the above

9. _____ became the leading force in moving Germany toward full unification in the 1980s.
    (a) Gustav Husak
    (b) Vaclav Havel
    (c) Janos Kada
    (d) Helmut Kohl

10. The agreement to recognize an independent Bosnia was signed in
    (a) Washington, D.C.
    (b) Gdansk.
    (c) Helsinki.
    (d) Dayton, Ohio.

True-False

_____ 1. In 1946 Winston Churchill delivered his famed "Iron Curtain" speech to a joint session of the Congress of the United States.

_____ 2. In enunciating the Truman Doctrine in 1947 the President implied that the United States would support free peoples against aggression everywhere in the world.

_____ 3. The concept of the "Iron Curtain" is associated with the Roosevelt administration.

_____ 4. Egyptian President Nasser in provoking the Middle East Crisis in 1956 was attempting to raise crude oil prices to support vast social programs in his own country.

_____ 5. Nationalist movements, colonial revolts, and Cold War politics are all factors in the so-called decolonization movement.

_____ 6. South Vietnamese President Diem and American President Kennedy were murdered in the same month.

_____ 7. American involvement in Southeast Asia throughout the 1960s allowed western European states to develop independently of American power and influence, and raised serious doubts about United States leadership of the free world.

_____ 8. The democratic socialist parties prospered after the onset of the Cold War.

_____ 9. The members of the Common Market sought to achieve the elimination of tariffs, a free flow of labor and capital, and similar wage and social benefits in all the participating countries.

_____ 10. Under President Jimmy Carter, the United States began a policy of détente with the Soviet Union.

Completion

1. The tense relationship between the United States and the Soviet Union began in the closing months of _____ .

2. The _____ was a program that provided broad economic aid to European states on the sole condition that they work together for their mutual benefit.

3. The murder of _____ was an early sign of communist intentions in Eastern Europe.

4. The 1955 formation of the _____ as an eastern-bloc military alliance demonstrated the extent of Cold war politics in Europe.

5. As early as 1917 the British government in issuing the _____ favored the establishment of a Jewish homeland in Palestine.

6. It would appear that the U.S. involvement in the early 1950s Korean conflict was interpreted by American policy makers as a success for the concept known as _____ .

7. The erection of the Berlin Wall occurred during the American presidency of _____ .

8. The defeat of the French forces in the battle of _____ effectively ended France's involvement in Indo-China.

9. President Richard Nixon's policy aimed at the gradual withdrawal of American combat forces from Vietnam was known as _____ .

10. Under the policy of _____ , Gorbachev proposed major economic and political reforms of the various centralized economic ministries.

Short Answer

1. In your opinion, how did the American response and policy development in respect to the Korean "police action" of 1950–1953 relate to later U.S. involvement in Vietnam?

2. Discuss the economic experiments sponsored under Nikita Khrushchev's leadership of the Soviet Union. Do these policies have a later effect? If so, discuss their implications in detail.

3. Describe the course of events in the post-World War II rivalry between the United States and the Soviet Union. Cite the significant examples of this superpower competition. What in your view led to the end of the Cold War?

4. What were the origins of the Indo-China conflict? Discuss the motivations of the major participants in that area's troubles over the thirty-year period beginning in 1945. Try to characterize the positions of each of the following countries: France, Russia, China, United States, South Vietnam, and North Vietnam.

Chapter 31
THE WEST AT THE DAWN OF THE TWENTY-FIRST CENTURY

Multiple-Choice

1. During the first half of the twentieth century the groups whose personal and social lives were most dramatically reshaped as a result of the radical transformations imposed by authoritarian governments were all of the following except
    - (a) women.
    - (b) children.
    - (c) Soviet peasants.
    - (d) Eastern European Jews.

2. The most significant postwar changes among Christian denominations have been in the
    - (a) Roman Catholic Church.
    - (b) Protestant Church.
    - (c) Anglican Church.
    - (d) Lutheran Church.

3. The immigration of Muslims into Western Europe arose from European economic growth and
    - (a) decolonization.
    - (b) discrimination.
    - (c) religious freedom.
    - (d) all of the above

4. The most important element of recent European feminism may be
    - (a) legal and civil equality with men.
    - (b) women controlling their own lives.
    - (c) better employment.
    - (d) none of the above

5. The intellectual movement that best captured the mood of mid-twentieth century European culture was
    - (a) intellectualism.
    - (b) romanticism.
    - (c) existentialism.
    - (d) classicism.

6. All of the following led to a marked change in how numerous Europeans thought about social welfare except
    - (a) decolonization.
    - (b) the rise of authoritarian states.
    - (c) World War II.
    - (d) The Great Depression.

7. The first European state to create a welfare state was
    (a) Germany.
    (b) Finland.
    (c) the United States.
    (d) Great Britain.

8. Simone de Beauvoir is the author of _____, a work that explored the difference being a woman had made in her life.
    (a) *Spare Rib*.
    (b) *Courage, Emma*.
    (c) *Women for Women*.
    (d) *The Second Sex*.

9. During the 1930s throughout Europe, students in the universities were often affiliated with what political party?
    (a) Communist Party
    (b) Democratic Party
    (c) Republican Party
    (d) none of the above

10. Which of the following philosophers was deeply compromised by his association with the Nazis?
    (a) Karl Jaspers
    (b) Martin Heidegger
    (c) Jean Paul Sartre
    (d) Albert Camus

True-False

_____1. The National Front, an extreme right-wing group that emerged in France, exploited the resentment of working-class voters toward North African immigrants.

_____2. Under communism Eastern European women rarely enjoyed social equality or government-financed benefits.

_____3. In the 1960s Turkish "guest workers" were invited to move to West Germany to fill a labor shortage that developed after World War II.

_____4. World War II created a refugee problem, and many people were displaced in central and Eastern Europe as well as the Soviet Union.

_____5. Student uprisings in the United States and Europe that began in the early 1960s were generally pro-military.

_____6. The expansion of consumerism in the West helped generate the discontent that brought down communist governments in Eastern Europe and the Soviet Union.

_____ 7. The Iranian Revolution of 1979 embodied the forces of what is commonly called Islamic *fundamentalism*.

_____ 8. Since World War II, the most widely read postwar work on women's issues was Simone de Beauvoir's *The Second Sex*.

_____ 9. Martin Heidegger was a major forerunner of existentialism.

_____ 10. American rock music is an example of the Americanization of European culture.

Completion

1. _____ led to the migration of many non-European inhabitants to Europe.

2. Both existentialists and romantic writers of the early nineteenth century questioned the primacy of _____.

3. The term _____ is often a term of criticism in European publications of the economic and military influence of the United States.

4. The Russian invasion of _____ in 1979 sought to impose a communist government on this Arab nation.

5. Before World War II, except in _____ , the two basic models for social legislation were the German and the British.

6. The decades since World War II have witnessed striking changes in the work patterns and social expectations of European women; as a result, more women have entered the _____ .

7. During the late 1920s and the 1930s, _____ became a substitute religion for some Europeans.

8. George Orwell expressed his disappointment with Stalin's policy in Spain in _____ .

9. The 1986 disaster at _____ heightened concern about environmental issues in the West.

10. The _____ movement originated among the radical student groups of the late 1960s and was concerned with the environment.

Short Answer

1. Discuss the internal and external forces that led to migration. What role did decolonization play.

2.. Discuss the intellectual movement known as existentialism. Who were some of the major writers who embraced this movement? How did their thoughts and writings reflect the happenings of the mid-twentieth century?

3. Discuss the emergence of concern for environmental issues in 1970s.

4. Describe the emergence of the computer and the changes this technology brought from its earliest inception to today.

5. Describe the emergence of radical political Islamism. What were the events that contributed to the rise of this movement?

LECTURE COMPANION

The following lecture note pages can be used to record your instructor's lectures and assignments for each chapter.

Chapter 13
PATHS TO CONSTITUTIONALISM AND ABSOLUTISM: ENGLAND AND FRANCE IN THE SEVENTEENTH CENTURY

Lecture Notes　　　　　　　　　　　　**Date:**_____

Chapter 14
NEW DIRECTIONS IN THOUGHT AND CULTURE IN THE SIXTEENTH AND SEVENTEENTH CENTURIES

Lecture Notes   **Date:**_____

Chapter 15
SUCCESSFUL AND UNSUCCESSFUL PATHS TO POWER
(1686–1740)

Lecture Notes   **Date:**_____

Chapter 16
SOCIETY AND ECONOMICS UNDER THE OLD REGIME IN THE EIGHTEENTH CENTURY

Lecture Notes **Date:**_____

Chapter 17
THE TRANSATLANTIC ECONOMY, TRADE WARS, AND COLONIAL REBELLION

Lecture Notes   **Date:** _____

Chapter 18
THE AGE OF ENLIGHTENMENT: EIGHTEENTH-CENTURY THOUGHT

Lecture Notes   **Date:** _____

Chapter 19
THE FRENCH REVOLUTION

Lecture Notes   **Date:**_____

Chapter 20
THE AGE OF NAPOLEON AND THE TRIUMPH OF ROMANTICISM

Lecture Notes   **Date:**_____

Chapter 21
THE CONSERVATIVE ORDER AND THE CHALLENGES OF REFORM (1815–1832)

Lecture Notes   **Date:**_____

Chapter 22
ECONOMIC ADVANCE AND SOCIAL UNREST
(1830–1850)

Lecture Notes   **Date:**_____

Chapter 23
THE AGE OF NATION-STATES

Lecture Notes   **Date:**_____

Chapter 24
THE BUILDING OF EUROPEAN SUPREMACY: SOCIETY AND POLITICS TO WORLD WAR I

Lecture Notes   **Date:**_____

Chapter 25
THE BIRTH OF MODERN EUROPEAN THOUGHT

Lecture Notes   **Date:**_____

Chapter 26
IMPERIALISM, ALLIANCES, AND WAR

Lecture Notes   **Date:**_____

Chapter 27
POLITICAL EXPERIMENTS OF THE 1920S

Lecture Notes Date:_____

Chapter 28
EUROPE AND THE GREAT DEPRESSION OF THE 1930S

Lecture Notes Date:_____

Chapter 29
WORLD WAR II

Lecture Notes   **Date:** _____

Chapter 30
THE COLD WAR ERA AND THE EMERGENCE OF THE NEW EUROPE

Lecture Notes Date:_____

Chapter 31
THE WEST AT THE DAWN OF THE TWENTY-FIRST CENTURY

Lecture Notes   **Date:**_____

ANSWER KEY

Chapter 13
Multiple-Choice
1. A
2. D
3. B
4. B
5. D
6. A
7. C
8. D
9. C
10. B

True-False
1. T
2. T
3. T
4. F
5. T
6. F
7. F
8. T
9. T
10. F

Completion
1. Mary Stuart, Queen of Scots
2. William Laud
3. Naseby
4. Marston Moor
5. Lord Protector
6. John Locke
7. corvee
8. parlements
9. Blaise Pascal
10. Mercantilism

Chapter 14
Multiple-Choice
1. D
2. A
3. D
4. A
5. A
6. C
7. D
8. C
9. B
10. A

True-False
1. T
2. F
3. T
4. T
5. T
6. T
7. F
8. T
9. F
10. T

Completion
1. Almagest
2. Johannes Kepler
3. mathematics
4. Isaac Newton
5. René Descartes
6. Thomas Hobbes
7. Francis Bacon
8. anarchy
9. Margaret Cavendish
10. John Locke

Chapter 15

Multiple-Choice
1. C
2. C
3. D
4. C
5. B
6. A
7. A
8. A
9. C
10. B

True-False
1. T
2. T
3. T
4. F
5. T
6. T
7. T
8. F
9. F
10. T

Completion
1. Spain
2. parlements
3. Cardinal Fleury
4. Robert Walpole
5. Vienna
6. Poland
7. Brandenburg
8. Junkers
9. Table of Ranks
10. Nikon

Chapter 16

Multiple-Choice
1. D
2. B
3. B
4. A
5. B
6. A
7. C
8. D
9. D
10. B

True-False
1. T
2. F
3. F
4. F
5. F
6. T
7. T
8. T
9. F
10. T

Completion
1. sword/robe
2. Charter of the Nobility
3. Land
4. Emelyan Pugachev
5. Thomas Newcomen
6. Henry Cort
7. London
8. William Hogarth
9. riots
10. Jews

Chapter 17
Multiple-Choice

1. B
2. B
3. C
4. A
5. D
6. C
7. D
8. C
9. C
10. B

True-False

1. F
2. T
3. T
4. F
5. T
6. F
7. F
8. T
9. T
10. T

Completion

1. Java
2. mercantilism
3. West Indies
4. Jenkins's Ear
5. French and Indian War
6. Sugar
7. Stamp Act
8. John Locke
9. George III
10. Whigs

Chapter 18
Multiple-Choice

1. A
2. B
3. C
4. B
5. A
6. C
7. A
8. A
9. C
10. B

True-False

1. T
2. F
3. F
4. T
5. T
6. F
7. F
8. F
9. F
10. F

Completion

1. England
2. The Spectator
3. Encyclopedia
4. deism
5. Edward Gibbon
6. Frederick the Great
7. Joseph II of Austria
8. German
9. Instructions
10. Poland

Chapter 19
Multiple-Choice
1. B
2. D
3. C
4. C
5. C
6. D
7. A
8. D
9. D
10. B

True-False
1. F
2. F
3. T
4. F
5. F
6. T
7. T
8. T
9. F
10. T

Completion
1. Louis XVI
2. voting or representation
3. seven
4. Pillnitz
5. Jacobins
6. Duke of Brunswick
7. Valmy
8. Edmund Burke
9. Bands of Jesus
10. Napoleon Bonaparte

Chapter 20
Multiple-Choice
1. C
2. D
3. C
4. C
5. C
6. D
7. A
8. A
9. D
10. B

True-False
1. F
2. T
3. F
4. F
5. T
6. F
7. T
8. F
9. F
10. F

Completion
1. Great Britain
2. Duke of Enghien
3. Austerlitz
4. Austrian Archduchess Marie Louise
5. Talleyrand
6. William Blake/Samuel T. Coleridge
7. Lord Byron
8. Faust
9. The Grimm Brothers
10. Georg W. F. Hegel

Chapter 21
Multiple-Choice
1. B
2. A
3. A
4. C
5. D
6. B
7. D
8. B
9. D
10. C

True-False
1. F
2. F
3. T
4. F
5. T
6. F
7. T
8. T
9. T
10. F

Completion
1. language
2. Enlightenment
3. Burchenschaften
4. Louis XVIII
5. Protocol of Troppau
6. Bernardo O'Higgins
7. Lyons
8. Leopold of Saxe-Coburg
9. Belgium
10. Catholic Emancipation

Chapter 22
Multiple-Choice
1. B
2. A
3. B
4. A
5. C
6. B
7. B
8. A
9. D
10. A

True-False
1. F
2. T
3. T
4. T
5. F
6. T
7. T
8. F
9. T
10. F

Completion
1. England or Wales
2. Feargus O'Connor
3. Thomas Malthus
4. Harriet Martineau
5. Robert Owen
6. Pierre Joseph Proudhon
7. Friedrich Engels
8. Karl Marx
9. Piedmont
10. unification

Chapter 23

Multiple-Choice
1. C
2. C
3. C
4. A
5. C
6. A
7. B
8. D
9. D
10. B

True-False
1. F
2. F
3. T
4. T
5. F
6. F
7. T
8. T
9. F
10. F

Completion
1. France
2. transformismo
3. Archduke Maximilian of Austria
4. Alfred Dreyfus
5. Emile Zola
6. Ausgleich or Compromise of 1867
7. zemstvos
8. Populism
9. Second Reform or Reform Bill of 1867
10. Charles Stewart Parnell

Chapter 24

Multiple-Choice
1. D
2. B
3. D
4. A
5. B
6. C
7. D
8. C
9. D
10. B

True-False
1. T
2. T
3. T
4. F
5. T
6. F
7. T
8. T
9. F
10. T

Completion
1. Germany
2. electricity
3. middle class
4. London
5. Opportunism
6. Eduard Bernstein
7. Sergei Witte
8. kulaks
9. Bolsheviks
10. Japan

Chapter 25

Multiple-Choice

1. C
2. B
3. B
4. B
5. C
6. A
7. A
8. C
9. A
10. B

True-False

1. T
2. F
3. T
4. T
5. F
6. T
7. F
8. F
9. F
10. T

Completion

1. Gregor Mendel
2. Herbert Spencer
3. Friedrich Nietzsche
4. Syllabus of Errors
5. Madame Bovary
6. Mrs. Warren's Profession
7. Virginia Woolf
8. Carl Jung
9. Max Weber
10. anti-Semitic

Chapter 26

Multiple-Choice

1. B
2. B
3. D
4. C
5. B
6. C
7. A
8. D
9. B
10. A

True False

1. F
2. T
3. T
4. T
5. T
6. F
7. F
8. T
9. T
10. F

Completion

1. J. A. Hobson
2. Otto von Bismarck
3. Three Emperors' League
4. Germany
5. Leo von Caprivi
6. Alfred von Tirpitz
7. Japan
8. Verdun, France
9. Russia or Soviet Union/Germany
10. France

Chapter 27

Multiple-Choice
1. D
2. C
3. B
4. A
5. C
6. A
7. C
8. B
9. D
10. C

True-False
1. F
2. T
3. T
4. T
5. F
6. F
7. T
8. F
9. T
10. T

Completion
1. Leon Trotsky
2. fascist
3. Victor Emmanuel III
4. Giacomo Matteotti
5. Lateran Accord
6. coalminers
7. Irish
8. Czechoslovakia
9. 800 million
10. Locarno

Chapter 28

Multiple-Choice
1. D
2. B
3. A
4. A
5. C
6. C
7. A
8. B
9. D
10. B

True-False
1. T
2. T
3. F
4. T
5. T
6. F
7. F
8. F
9. T
10. F

Completion
1. Herbert Hoover
2. John Maynard Keynes
3. National Government
4. Hindenburg Circle
5. Reichstag Fire
6. President Hindenburg
7. Heinrich Himmler
8. Nuremburg Laws
9. Ethiopia
10. Collectivization

Chapter 29

Multiple-Choice
1. D
2. D
3. D
4. D
5. A
6. B
7. A
8. C
9. D
10. D

True-False
1. T
2. F
3. T
4. T
5. T
6. T
7. T
8. T
9. F
10. F

Completion
1. Poland/Ukraine
2. memories
3. Francisco Franco
4. appeasement
5. *untermenschen*
6. *Judenrein*
7. Coral Sea
8. Stalingrad
9. Tehran, Iran
10. Josef Stalin

Chapter 30

Multiple-Choice
1. D
2. B
3. C
4. C
5. C
6. C
7. D
8. A
9. D
10. D

True-False
1. F
2. T
3. F
4. F
5. T
6. T
7. T
8. F
9. T
10. F

Completion
1. World War II
2. Marshall Plan
3. Jan Masaryk
4. Warsaw Pact
5. Balfour Declaration
6. containment
7. John F. Kennedy
8. Dien Bien Phu
9. Vietnamization
10. perestroika

Chapter 31

Multiple-Choice

1. B	6. A
2. A	7. D
3. A	8. D
4. B	9. A
5. C	10. B

True-False

1. T	6. T
2. F	7. T
3. T	8. T
4. T	9. F
5. F	10. T

Completion

1. Decolonization
2. reason
3. Americanization
4. Afghanistan
5. Scandinavia
6. "learning professions"
7. Communism
8. Homage to Catalonia
9. Chernobyl
10. German Green